ORIGAMI

ORIGAMI

THE ART OF PAPERFOLDING

ROBERT HARBIN

HarperPerennial

A Division of HarperCollins*Publishers*

To Neal Elias and Fred Rohm

This book was originally published by The English Universities Press, Ltd. under the title *Teach Yourself Origami.*

ORIGAMI. Copyright © 1969 by Robert Harbin. All rights reserved. Printed in the United States of America. No part of this book may be used or reproduced in any manner whatsoever without written permission except in the case of brief quotations embodied in critical articles and reviews. For information address HarperCollins Publishers, Inc., 10 East 53rd Street, New York, NY 10022.

HarperCollins books may be purchased for educational, business, or sales promotional use. For information, please call or write: Special Markets Department, HarperCollins Publishers, Inc., 10 East 53rd Street, New York, NY 10022. Telephone: (212) 207-7528; Fax: (212) 207-7222.

First BARNES & NOBLE BOOKS edition published 1979.
First HarperPerennial edition published 1992.

LIBRARY OF CONGRESS CATALOG CARD NUMBER 91-55514

ISBN 0-06-092269-9

95 96 97 98 ❖/RRD H 10 9 8 7 6 5 4

PREFACE

Writing a book, whatever the subject, is always a laborious task for me. But writing this one has been a real pleasure, because I am anxious to introduce as many as possible to this new world of Origami which has given me so much enjoyment.

The main task has been to design the illustrations, because without them there could not be a book. Diagrams take a long time to prepare because, fold by fold, the three-dimensional paper model must be reduced to a two-dimensional drawing on a flat sheet of paper. And the drawing must be clear and accurate if the student is to understand how to produce the finished model from it.

It could be argued, I suppose, that Origami has an end product that is not worth keeping. Nothing could be further from the truth. At the time of writing, I have a delightful collection of the world's best paper folds, carefully stored in transparent envelopes, which are in turn mounted on a sheet of black board. This way, they are ready to be produced and shown quickly—and they *are* produced and shown, at the slightest provocation!

If this art form captures you, as it has certainly captured me and many others, you will discover that it brings with it a new dimension in enjoyment, which is infinite in its variety and unrivalled in its capacity to make you relax and forget everything else.

London   ROBERT HARBIN

CONTENTS

A SHORT HISTORY
OF ORIGAMI

'Origami' (pronounced *or-i-gäm'ē*) is a Japanese word which means paper-folding. The Japanese do not consider Origami to be an art form, but look on it rather as something which is an integral part of their culture.

Associated in the first instance with the making of intricate paper dolls, the designing of *Noshis* (folded tokens) and of attractive packaging, Origami has now become an accepted pastime for the young and an intellectual hobby for many adults.

In Japan, two great names dominate the Origami scene: Akira Yoshizawa and Okimasa Uchiyama. The genius of Yoshizawa has influenced most Japanese and Western folders.

Because of the sudden interest the West has shown in Origami, Japanese publishers have been quick to produce a flood of attractive books on the art, written in Japanese and English, and many of them containing complete finished models pasted into the books themselves.

Although these Japanese books are a delight to look at, they fail in the object of teaching. Westerners do not easily follow diagrams, and the Japanese wrongly assume that their explanations are sufficient instruction for the beginner.

Peter Van Note, of New York, who is a keen paper-folder, has carried out some research on the origins of Origami, and has the following observations to make: 'I recently acquired, by pure chance, a Japanese manuscript describing paper-folding according to the ancient practices. It was published about the same time as the Kan No Mado manuscript, but I have reason to believe that it illustrates the paper-folding of Japan's Heian Period (A.D. 782–1185).

'If this is proven true (and I believe it can be), then we

have the earliest examples of paper-folding on record—
about 1,000 years old.

'In the Japanese way of figuring time, the aforementioned
manuscript dates back to the middle of the Edo Period,
which lasted from about the time England's Henry Hudson
was sailing up the Hudson River (1607–1611) to shortly
after the American Civil War (1865).

'For what it is worth, here is a thumbnail outline of the
history of Origami:

Elaborate ceremonial paper-folding and simple "re-
creational" paper-folding—Heian Period.

Water Bomb Base: probably used in the Heian Period
for making ceremonial paper butterfly figures.

Crane Base (Bird Base): Edo Period, probably 1700's
to mid-1800's.

Frog Base: Late Edo Period, probably not before the
1800's.

'The above conclusions must necessarily be tentative, but
they are based on good evidence. It should be noted that
the Heian and Edo Periods were times of peace and leisure
in Japanese history, while the intervening four centuries
were characterised by instability and bloody battle.'

Thank you, Peter Van Note!

The Spanish have been great paper-folders for many
years, and the best Western results have emerged from
Spain and the Argentine. You should watch out for names
like Vicente Solorzano, Ligia Montoya, N. Doctor Montero,
and many more. The Spanish have a style of their own, of
which the Praying Moor figure (included in this book) is a
fine example.

In Great Britain, things are beginning to happen these
days, and some fine originals are appearing. Look out for
names like Eric Kenneway, Iris Walker, and Trevor
Hatchett and Tim Ward, two brilliant young men from
Oxford University. These two enthusiasts are busily preparing a book about their own creations which they hope to
have published in the near future.

By far the most exciting results are coming from America, and you will come across names like Fred Rohm, Neal Elias, Robert Neale, George Rhoads, Jack Skillman, and many others, both male and female. Many books would need to be written to keep pace with the flood of originals coming from this source.

Mrs. Lillian Oppenheimer, of New York, has devoted a great part of her life to stimulating interest in Origami, and to this end she runs an Origami Centre in New York, and is the publisher of *The Origamian*, which keeps the dedicated enthusiasts in touch with current Origami happenings.

I am happy to include in this book several originals by contemporary folders from many countries, and to them I tender my grateful thanks.

THE ESSENTIALS
OF ORIGAMI

It is a fact that most beginners are not able to follow diagrams and instructions easily and successfully, however carefully they may have been planned. As a rule, Origami illustrators try to cram into each page as much information as possible. This practice is welcomed by the enthusiast and the expert, because it means that the book will be able to explain a large number of models. Unfortunately, though, a page filled with diagrams completely bewilders most beginners.

I have borne this in mind while preparing this book, and you will notice that the earlier pages have been designed with no more than two or three diagrams per page. All the diagrams are clearly drawn, and contain helpful instructions and symbols to give you all possible help, and to explain the mainly standard models which bring you in touch with most of the Basic Folds.

A Basic Fold is a fold from which many models can be made. There are many Basic Folds, both ancient and modern, but this book will introduce you to just enough to give you a good groundwork on which to begin.

Look at the first fold illustrated in the book, and notice how the instructions are placed on the parts to be folded: FOLD THIS SIDE DOWN, and then TO HERE, and so on. The instructions are made to work for you. Later in the book, the instructions are placed alongside the diagrams, and not on them, because it is assumed that by then you will have become familiar with the different processes.

Always fold carefully, accurately, and neatly. If you fold carelessly, the result will be disastrous.

Study each diagram showing the complete folded model. Then, and only then, place your Origami paper in front of you and make your first fold.

When you make a fold, always crease the paper firmly with the back of your thumbnail. Good creases make folding easy, and are an invaluable guide later in the model, when you are making a series of folds.

Pre-creasing is an important feature. Consider, for example, the Japanese Lady. This model was sent to Samuel Randlett, who immediately used the idea to produce his fine Fish. Notice how he pre-creases the paper he uses so that everything folds into place at the right moment.

Before you make a Reverse Fold, pre-crease the paper by folding the whole thickness before opening the paper and making the fold (see Reverse Folds).

Notice how paper coloured on one side is used to get the maximum effect for each model. The subject of paper is an important one. Origami paper (which is available from a variety of sources, some of which I have listed at the end of this book) should be strong, thin, and suitably coloured. But if you cannot lay hands on special Origami paper, almost any paper may be used.

If you are instructed to use a square of paper, make sure that it really is square, and that a rectangle is a true rectangle. Most of the models in this book are based on squares of paper, but there is no regular rule about this, as all shapes of paper can be used, according to the model's needs. See, for example, the Ornithonimus and Aladdin's Lamp.

Origami is not meant to be a simple art. To the expert, it is a challenge to the eye, the brain, and the fingers, a wonderful mental and physical therapy.

When you fold one of the decorations explained in this book, you will find that by altering this or that fold you can invent endless shapes. In fact, you can doodle for hours.

When you have mastered the Basic Folds, you will then be equipped to produce figures and shapes of your own. Have something in mind, and then consider the best Base from which to start. You will notice that there are three different ways in which to make a Penguin. The Penguin seems to be a favourite subject, and almost every folder has had a go at it.

Watch out for terms like Squash Fold. It is so named because you do just that—squash the part indicated so that the sides bulge and it flattens, in most cases symmetrically.

Study the Petal Folds, the Rabbit's Ears, and the various Bases, and try to remember what they are. If you get stuck, have a look at the Contents and refer to the page or pages concerned.

You will notice that certain procedures are used over and over again. You will soon get used to these and be able to carry them out automatically.

When you have folded everything in the first half of the book, you will find that more and more diagrams begin to appear on each page, and that the symbols begin to play a bigger part than the instructions. Decoration 2 has been included as an exercise so try to make this up using the symbols only.

Start at the beginning of the book and work your way slowly and steadily through. Do not attempt anything too difficult, to start with, because this can only end in disappointment.

If you are making a long train journey, take this book with you and fold a piece of paper to pass the time during your journey. Find a friend with the same interest, and you will both pass many a happy hour.

For the rehabilitation of damaged hands there is nothing like Origami for making reluctant fingers come back to life.

Finally—take it slowly; fold carefully, neatly and accurately. And START AT THE BEGINNING.

A Note on
SYMBOLS

The symbols used in this book are based on Akira Yoshizawa's code of lines and arrows. Symbols must become second nature to you when folding, but you will find that they are easy to acquire.

The moment you see a line of dashes, you know that the paper must be Valley Folded along that line. When you see a line of dashes and dots, you recognise the sign for a Mountain Fold. To make a Mountain Fold, you naturally turn the paper upside down and make a Valley Fold.

Arrows show the directions in which you must fold: left, right, up, down, in front, behind, and into.

You will notice one arrow which shows that a drawing has been enlarged for clarity. Another arrow indicates that a model must be opened out (see Samuel Randlett's Fish). My own special little black arrow indicates that you must sink, press, squeeze, or push in at certain points.

The symbols are in fact self-explanatory. They are simple common sense, and can be learnt in about ten minutes.

Try to use the symbols only and ignore explanations. This will help you when you come to read Japanese Origami books.

**valley fold
a series of dashes**

**means fold
like this**

**mountain fold
a series of dashes
and dots**

**means fold
like this**

if a drawing
was marked
with these symbols

the result
should be
this

when a drawing
is followed by
this little looped
arrow

turn the
model over
so

this black arrow

means push in

thin lines mean creases

this symbol

means

fold over and
over

MAKE THIS WATER BOMB BASE AND PRELIMINARY FOLD

if a drawing is
marked like this

you make this
water bomb base

if you turn this
fold inside out
you will get this

preliminary fold

reverse fold 1

crease

note how paper is
marked. crease
along the mark.
now reverse fold
as shown

like
this

and this

reverse fold 2

crease

note how paper is
marked. crease
along the mark.
now reverse fold
as shown

how to fold feet.
(birds, animals, people.)
1. reverse fold 2
2. reverse fold 1
3. two reverse folds

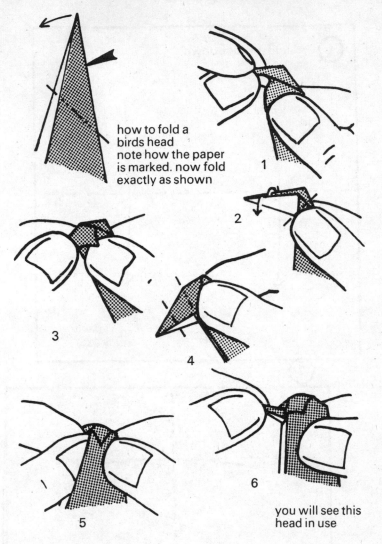

how to fold a
birds head
note how the paper
is marked. now fold
exactly as shown

1

2

3

4

5

6

you will see this
head in use

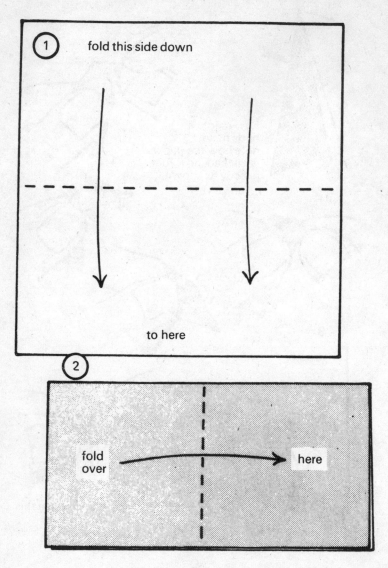

① fold this side down

to here

② fold over → here

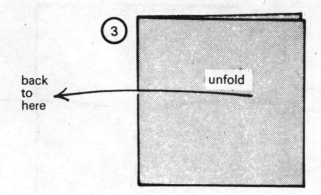

③ back to here ← unfold

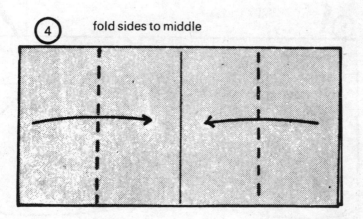

④ fold sides to middle

like this

and this

a squash fold

now draw doors and windows

fold
flap

this
inside

now –
turn the
model over

like this

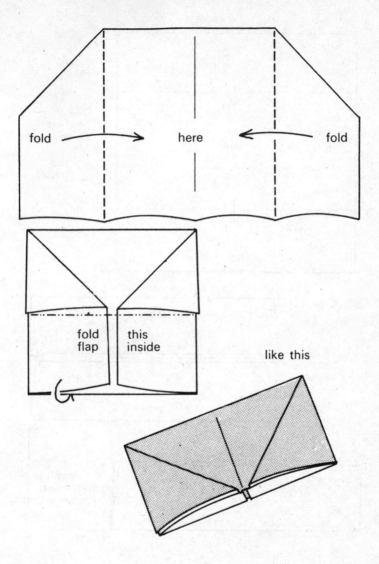

fold ———→ here ←——— fold

fold flap | this inside

like this

BOAT *Use a square of paper*

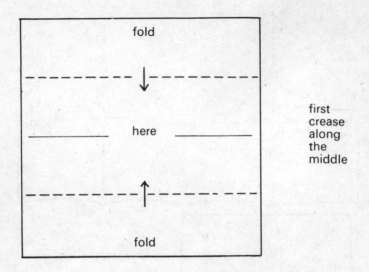

first
crease
along
the
middle

like this

now fold
the two
corners up

like
this

fold here

fold behind

and behind

fold down

like this

crease along marked lines

and flatten bottom

the boat

③ now fold the corners in

④ like this

25

5 fold the corners in

6 like this

turn over

squeeze into shape

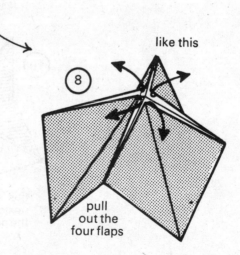

like this

pull
out the
four flaps

9 like this

the salt cellar

10

this is the salt cellar
upside down. colour
the areas shown

⑪ to make
the colour
changer

⑫ and this
shows how you
make it work

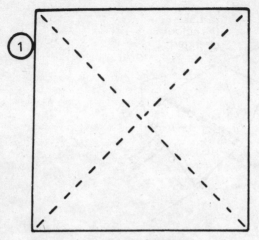

crease along the marked lines

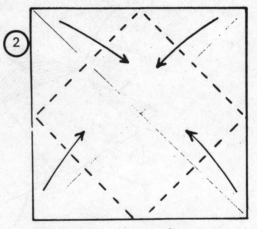

fold the four corners to the centre

so

③

turn
over

④

fold
four
corners
to the centre

31

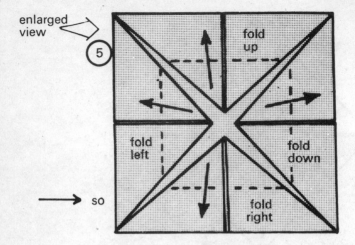

enlarged view

5

fold up

fold left

fold down

fold right

so

6

turn over

so

completed pleats

push left thumb into each
corner and press together
on the outside until the
fancy box is completed

so

fill the box with sweets

35

fold this side down

here

fold flap down

turn over

fold corners in

like this

fold this flap over
twice

now fold this
flap under twice

fold and tuck sides into
pockets

7 like this

turn over

8

fold down top and tuck into pocket

9 like this

turn over

the turban complete

try this with
a sheet of
newspaper

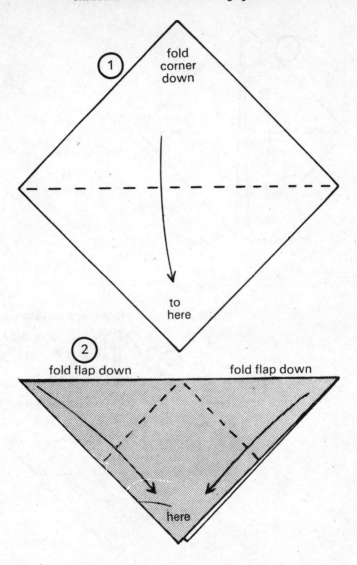

① fold
corner
down

to
here

② fold flap down   fold flap down

here

③ like this

fold these flaps up

like this

④ fold these two points outwards see ⑤

fold this flap up

like this

⑤

fold this flap up

⑥

so

fold this flap behind

43

7

A

B

squash corners together

like
this

8

B

A

turn these
two corners
up in front
and behind

44

(9)

like
this
now open
up again as
in (7)

a piece of paper
20 inches square
will make a hat
to fit your head

like this

1

crease
along
marked lines

2

fold four corners
to the centre

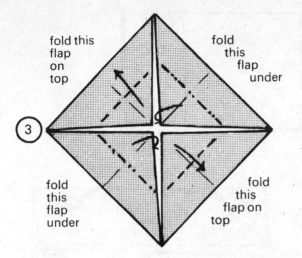

fold this
flap
on
top

fold
this
flap
under

③

fold
this
flap
under

fold
this
flap on
top

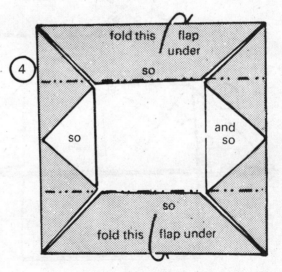

④

fold this flap
under

so

so

and
so

so

fold this flap under

⑤ flaps
folded
behind,
now turn
over

⑥ fold the
four

corners
inwards

so

⑦

fold the
four corner
flaps inwards

48

⑧

fold flap down

fold flap up

⑨

so

open up the
middle

⑩

so

turn over

press thumbs in, then
with fingers pull
sides up – and so
turn the boat
inside out – the
result will be
this

③

fold in
the creases

④   so

fold the two corners
to the bottom

fold the two corners behind

fold the two flaps
to the centre

53

fold the two
flaps behind

fold
these
small
flaps up

do
the
same
behind

tuck
these
flaps into
pockets

do
the
same
behind

⑩ like this

⑪ hold the model like this

blow in here

the water bomb completed

⑫

1 crease along marked lines

2 and fold corners to centre
then turn over

3 here ← fold corner over

squash
point
flat

4a

lift
flap
up

4

so

turn over

5

6

lift flap
up

squash point
flat, see
fig. 4a & 5

⑦

⑧

open
out
X
and
Y

lift
A
up

A

Y

⑨

turn
over

A

X

open out X and Y

lift
A
up
as
in
fig.
8
and
9

⑬

fold
back
flap
down
also

fold
flap

this
down

⑭ so

now open out

so

① crease along
marked
lines

and
then   turn
over

so

② now
crease
these
along
marked
lines

③ pull
the
corners
together

④ A so

lift A

open   out

⑤ so

A

half
open

repeat on
other
side

6

opened
squashed

and
flat

A

7

lift

flap

8

so, and repeat
on other
side

squash   corners

63

9 fold flaps on top and underneath

so

10 fold corners   fold corners

11 fold   fold   here here   fold   fold

repeat behind

64

12

so

pull top
flaps down

13

so

14

crease
along the
marked lines
then turn over

crease
marked

along
lines

and then fold up

so

push thumbs
together
until
they meet

so

now look at
fig. 5

67

⑤ fold down

fold down behind

here

⑥ make the handle

⑦ like this

68

⑧ fold handle in

⑨ handle folded into model in front and behind

⑩ now fold four corners into model

pull out

pull out

⑪

push flaps in

⑫

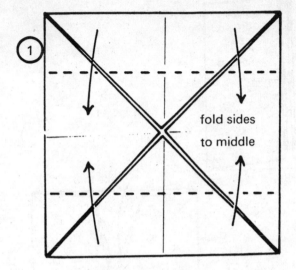

fold sides
to middle

like this

fold sides to the middle

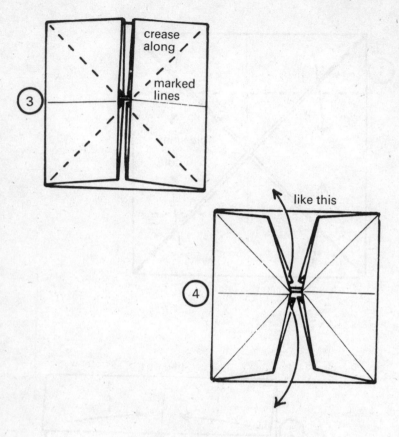

crease
along

marked
lines

③

like this

④

now pull out the
two arrowed
points, the creases
will guide you and
they will fall into
place as in fig. 5

like
this

⑤

now pull
out these
two points

like
this

⑥

fold
flaps
along
marked line

to make this
windmill

fold the
model in half
backwards
see fig. 8

⑦

⑧

to make
this
vase

now fold this
flap

to make this
boat with sail

now start at fig. 6
and fold the model
in half to
make this
catamaran

fold behind

fold behind

pull
open

pull
open

so

③

squash flat

so

④

p
u
l
l

o
u
t

p
u
l
l

o
u
t

hold
like this
and form
gondola

like this

squash
this
flap

here the flap
is seen half
squashed

completely
squashed

turn over

82

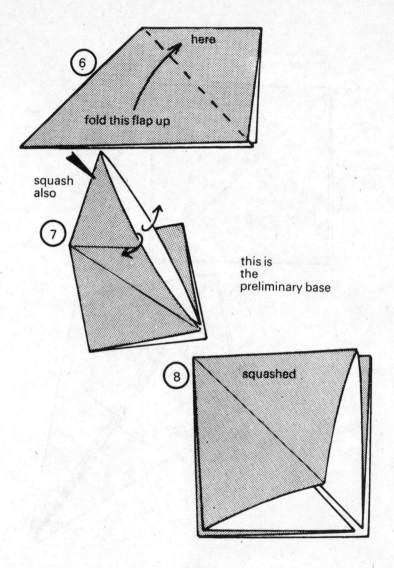

6 here

fold this flap up

squash
also

7

this is
the
preliminary base

8 squashed

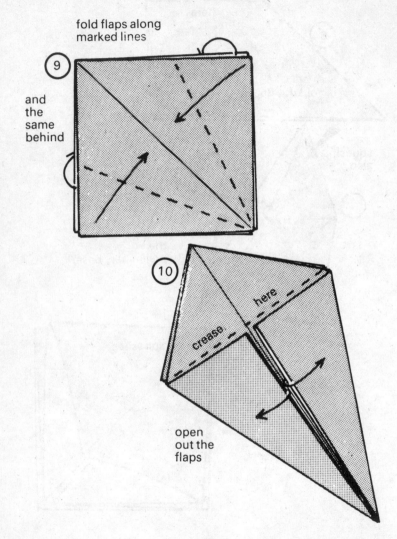

fold flaps along
marked lines

⑨

and
the
same
behind

⑩

here

crease

open
out the
flaps

lift this flap up

this is how
you hold the
flap

⑬ press flat

⑭ so

now turn over
and repeat
folds with
the other
side

this is
the bird
base

1 start with
the bird
base

reverse
fold this
point

2

so

③ and so

④ finally so

now reverse fold this point

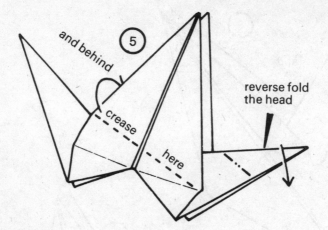

⑤ and behind

crease —— here

reverse fold the head

⑥

pull the tail – the wings will flap

PIGEON *Akira Yoshizawa, Tokio, Japan*

Start With
Bird Base

1

reverse
fold both
these legs

2

but
reverse
fold
only
as far
as this

open up the leg flaps

91

fold all four sides
to the centre line
to make legs

like
this

now fold the
top flaps down to complete legs

like
this

5

fold this flap down

6

fold this
flap under

93

fold this flap
down and
up

⑦

⑧

A

fold A
under
to B
so folding
the model
in half

B

pull neck
back

like this

(9)

reverse
fold
both legs
backwards

A

B

(10)

fold
breast
flaps
in

reverse fold
the tail

reverse fold the legs

95

11

reverse
fold the
head

fold
head
flaps
down

now form
beak

reverse
fold
feet

reverse fold
the tail again

fold in

fold in

and again

fold
backwards
and
forwards

hold   hold

flatten out
the top and
then 'sink' the
middle

and then
press flat

A
B

so

now form
a rabbit's
ear
with
A and
with
B

fold flaps
A and B
upwards

A

B

reverse   fold

squash A + B
flat
both sides

reverse fold
this point

reverse fold
here

fold
arms
both
sides

reverse fold foot

form
head

form
hands

reverse fold
twice

head
and
beard

fold
arms

THE PRAYING MOOR
COMPLETED

⑦ D C

then
squash
flat

⑧ like
this

D

lift
flap
up

C

like this

⑨ D

squash
flat

like
this

⑩ pull D
up here

D

fold
side
in

fold
side in

like
this

(11)

D

do
the
same
with
the 3
other
sides

like
this

D

(12)

now
move to
the next page

fold
top
flap
over

here

so

here

fold

fold

17

fold
here
and behind

18

reverse fold

reverse fold

so

19

so

turn
over

now reverse
fold
all tips

blow

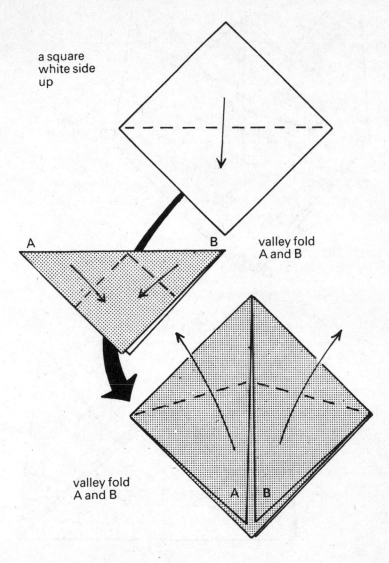

a square
white side
up

valley fold
A and B

valley fold
A and B

III

fold
C in front
B behind

D C

C
rabbits' ear

make eyes with gummed eyelets

① fold fold here

② so turn over

③ so fold in half

114

4

so

pull down
and flatten

fold down
behind

5

6

fold
model
in
half

this
is
the
<u>fish</u>
<u>base</u>

so

so

7 so lift corner upright

squash

8 and this corner too

reverse fold both points

9 so

10 so

tuck flaps
under and
in

11 so

pull down
front and
back

12 so

13 reverse fold points

14 now form heads

turn
over

hold
points
A – B

A

B

pull firmly

C

you are
making a
stretched bird
base

like
this

A

D

B

bring C   D together press flat

119

B

reverse
fold B
when
C + D are
folded

shape
head

the
flippers
will
be
pulled
down

C

D

fold
this
thin
flap
front
and
back

make
rabbit's
ears
with
C ÷ D

reverse
fold

reverse
fold

B

sink corners, a
water bomb base

use a square, crease
diagonals
fold
down

fold single flap
down
and squash

fold model in half

so

fold flap down
then fold over
and over three
times

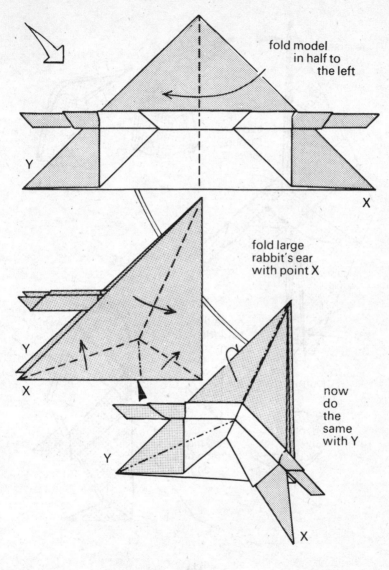

fold model
in half to
the left

fold large
rabbit's ear
with point X

now
do
the
same
with Y

reverse
fold
head

fold
flippers
forward

make tail
of hidden
point

X   Y
form   feet

(see mother
hubbard's
dog)

RABBIT   *Michael P. Guy, Birmingham, England*

begin with
stretched
bird base

A and B
rabbit's ears

cut
X and Y
single
layer

reverse fold

open out
under
cheeks

form head

125

RABBIT *Using stretched Bird Base (see Penguin I)*

round
body
off

TROPICAL BIRD I   *Ligia Montoya, Argentina.*
Fish Base

fold
in half
behind

so

squash

so

lift
up

repeat
on other
side

fold
here

fold sides
in for legs

and   behind

start forming head

reverse
fold
chest

push in
chest

fold
shoulders
in

reverse
fold feet

reverse fold
tail

fold
tail
in

form
the
beak

push in

reverse
fold
feet

fold tail
tips in
both sides

129

reverse fold
the neck

crease
neck
along
marked
line
then
push
in

crimp
the tail

so

fold stomach
in both sides

fold tail in

reverse
fold
neck

form
beak

fold
stomach
again

start
like
this

then
fold
sides
in

like
this

fold
lower
flap up

so

now fold
the lower
flap
twice

like
this

then
turnover

132

fold
point
up

like this

now fold
sides in
and squash
corners

fold
behind

so

fold flap down

now fold
flap up
and push
sides in
so

now fold
flap into
model

fold

fold

so

tree
swings
back

133

note how the
flap locks
the 'tub'

fold
tree

so

fold   fold

so

turn over

XMAS
TREE

use a square

fold flaps in

fold point

then fold in half

form muzzle of dog

form tail

crimp neck

A

one, crease a square of paper into thirds, and down the diagonal

two, fold A behind to crease only

B

C

petal fold A (see bird base)

three, fold B + C to the middle and squash A

A

B   C

crease and push in or 'sink' sides

A

C

B

turn cloak inside out and put thumbs in here fingers gripping behind hat

136

X

X
hold

fold
back this
portion

now repeat
with the
other
side

begin to
form hand
watch X

form
hand
watch X

tuck
in
X

X

X

X

hold by
shoulders

crease
and sink
shoulders
Y will move
forward

Y

watch Y

reverse
fold bonnet

Y

fold Y
inside like this

fold   in
bottom flaps

138

bonnet
reversed

reverse
fold tip of
bonnet

(mother
hubbard's
dog explained
elsewhere)

FRIAR TUCK *Eric Kenneway, London*

use a square

crease carefully

A → B

then fold A over to B

C will move

C

reverse fold point

A

B

C

sink

see praying moor

½

crimp in front and behind

fold flap up in front & behind

H

fold point in (see m. hubbard)

crimp point inside

sink points fold flaps

reverse fold face

fold here

fold behind

form hand

H

H

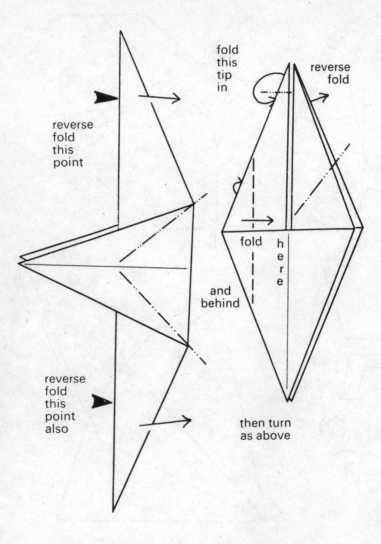

reverse
fold
this
point

fold
this
tip
in

reverse
fold

reverse
fold
this
point
also

fold

h
e
r
e

and
behind

then turn
as above

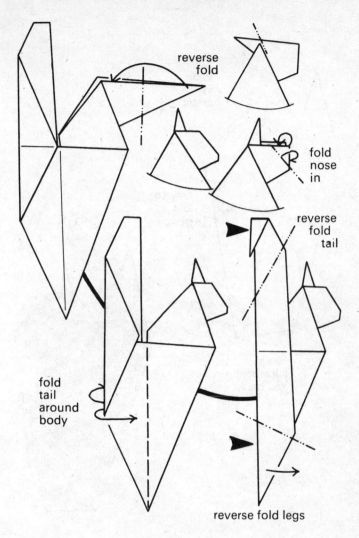

reverse fold

fold nose in

reverse fold tail

fold tail around body

reverse fold legs

fold
in
chest

reverse
fold
paws

fold in
flaps front
and back

144

PRINTER'S HAT *Al Koenig and Mike Moarako, U.S.A.*

fold

newspaper

here

fold

fold top
flap only

distance
between
A and B
is the
size
of

turn
over

your
head

fold

A

here

B

here

fold corners
under

now fold
flap over
twice

open out
until A and B
meet

fold
in

A

using thumbs
open out
the hat
until A and B
meet

B

A

bring A and B
together

fold in

A

B

fold in

A

B

now open
out again
and put on hat

DECORATION I *Robert Harbin, London, see Multiform*

lift
and
squash
fold
each
corner

like this

press
flat

fold
in
eight
flaps

treat
A and B
C and D
as
bird
bases

B

nearly
there

these
are known
as
<u>petal folds</u>

A

half
way

D

C

started

complete

148

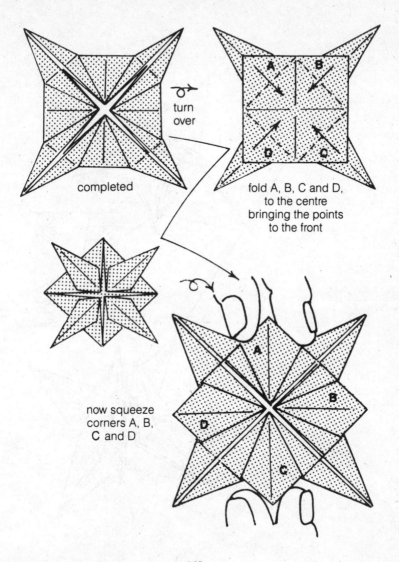

turn over

completed

fold A, B, C and D,
to the centre
bringing the points
to the front

now squeeze
corners A, B,
C and D

149

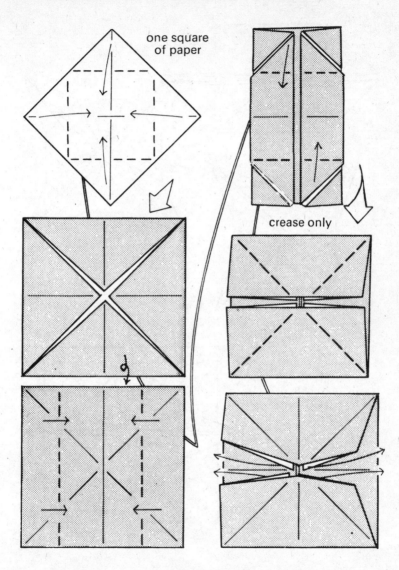

one square
of paper

crease only

a little help!
pull out flaps
A, B, C and D

well
did
you
do
it ?

if you
sink
corners
A, B, C and D
you can
then pull
out base
and make
a fine
fancy
box

make diagonal creases

double
fold

here

fold

form
head

here

fold   fold

here

fold
flap
behind

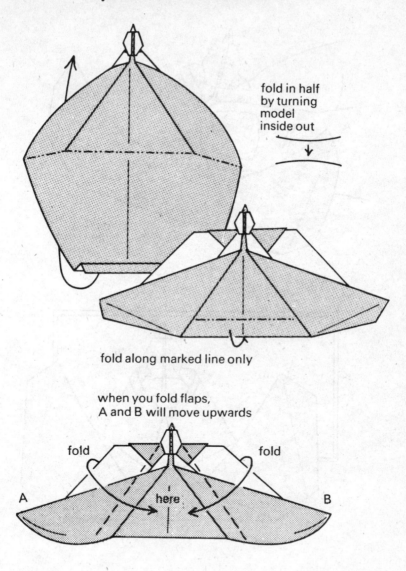

fold in half
by turning
model
inside out

fold along marked line only

when you fold flaps,
A and B will move upwards

fold   fold

A   here   B

A

B

then press
flat

here

fold   fold

allow rear flaps
to come in front

fold behind

pull A over to B
carefully

now reserve fold
A over left, then
treat B as A

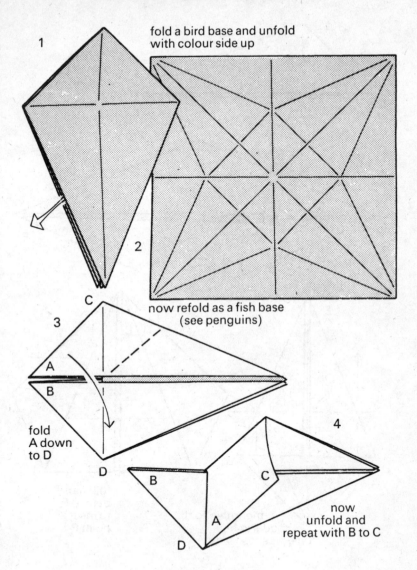

1

fold a bird base and unfold
with colour side up

2

now refold as a fish base
(see penguins)

3

C

A
B

fold
A down
to D

D

4

B   C

A

D

now
unfold and
repeat with B to C

5   now fold
F over to
the left

F

E

open out F

6

F

E

E   7

mountain fold
model in half
(see japanese lady)

F

F

8

E

P

fold flap F
behind F
to meet
point P

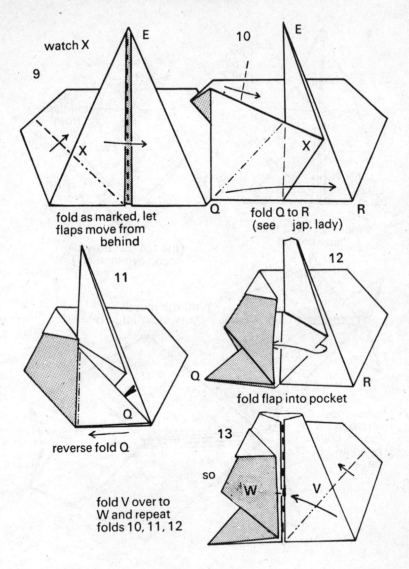

9

watch X

E

fold as marked, let
flaps move from
behind

10

E

X

Q   R

fold Q to R
(see   jap. lady)

11

Q

reverse fold Q

12

Q   R

fold flap into pocket

13

so

W   V

fold V over to
W and repeat
folds 10, 11, 12

163

14 Z
open out
flaps
pull Z
down

mountain fold tail
flaps behind

Z
fold
tail flaps
front
tips flip
behind

15

(the tail can now be
made symmetrical)

16
Z
form the mouth
— now blow into body

press top
and bottom
mouth will
open and
close

crease   first

angles   equal

cut diamond from 4 x 3
rectangle

form
this
shape

M
fold

head

fore
legs

leg   leg

tail

cut both sides
of middle for legs

the tail

open tail to make
crimps

the head and neck

open
out

back legs

reverse fold

166

fore legs

Fold preliminary base behind

Fold preliminary base in front

A rectangle cut as shown (gold side under)

Form two bird bases one on top of the other

so

Joined here. Now study the next page carefully

Rearrange the Bird Bases so

Fold Whole Base Down

Joined

so

Fold and Hold

Now Fold White Base up

Sink Base see next page

hold

Make White Stretched Bird Base

fold back a into itself
(back
view)   so

b

sink
corner into genie

R. fold

b

fold arms
down

crimp
genie
both
sides

reverse
fold
points
but not
genie

b

crimp
genie
again

a

M fold
flaps
for
handle

V. fold

R. fold
handle

reverse fold
head

b

b

R. fold
hands

fold
into pocket

form
lamp
handle

b

hat
locked

now
fold
this
side
into
pocket

fold in one side
of hat
so

OSTRICH *Robert Harbin, London. Begin with Bird Base*

make rabbit's ear

fold front flap up

rabbit's ear

fold in half behind

lift legs A B upright

A

B

and then squash

crease along valley lines only, front and back

X   Y

now twist A inside so that X + Y change places also B

B   A

reverse
tail

first
fold in
leg flaps

then
fold
these
flaps

first
fold leg
flaps
front &
back

form
legs of
man as
above

form rabbit's ear
make creases only

R.
fold

R. fold
legs
and
form
feet

now
fold
this

like this

reverse
fold both
legs

R.
fold
head

form
body
and
head

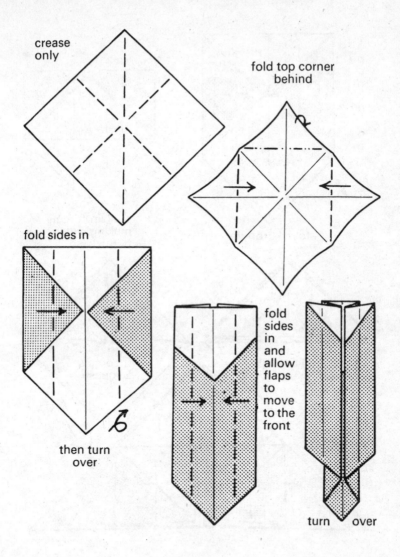

crease
only

fold top corner
behind

fold sides in

then turn
over

fold
sides
in
and
allow
flaps
to
move
to the
front

turn   over

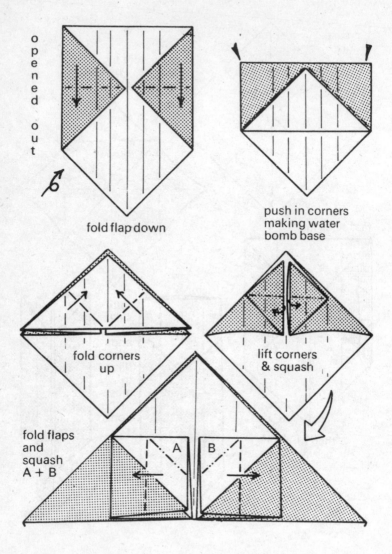

opened out

fold flap down

push in corners
making water
bomb base

fold corners
up

lift corners
& squash

fold flaps
and
squash
A + B

A   B

176

fold
up
X

when folded hold X
and pull point Y

X

Y

when thumbs meet
model will fold into
place

press
model
into creases
and move
thumb and
finger to front

Y

reverse fold Y
and fold top
flap to the left

Y

open
out
and
lift Y
up

Y

Y

Y

fold flaps in

crimp
spire then
fold behind

fold
spire
edges

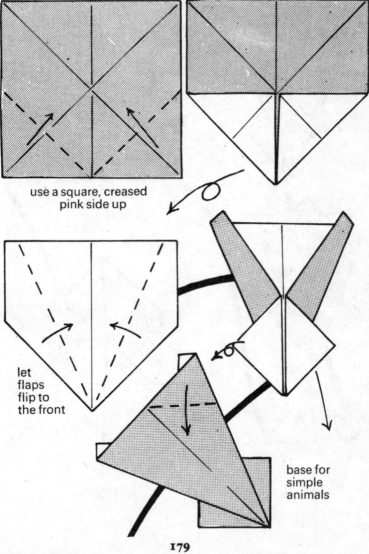

use a square, creased
pink side up

let
flaps
flip to
the front

base for
simple
animals

repeat
folds
with
A

A

flap behind
flips to front

fold top flat
down

tail

fold model
in
half

pull
tail
down

crimp
neck

reverse
fold
trunk

form
trunk

fold
in

crimp
chin

begin with a
bird base

fold
flaps
front
and
back

reverse fold
inside points
either side
of middle
point

reverse fold middle point

squash fold
B and C

reverse fold
A and D

C

B

A

D

fold top edges of B and C
inwards

petal fold
B and C

tuck in flaps to lock
base

A and D

184

BIBLIOGRAPHY

Here are the titles of a few books on Origami, which are fairly easy to obtain.

HARBIN, Robert. *Secrets of Origami*, Oldbourne Press, London (1963). One hundred and fifty models are explained by 1,400 drawings and 70 photographs. The standard line-and-arrow code is used. The world's leading folders have contributed original models to this anthology, which also contains a large selection of traditional folds.

— *Paper Magic*, Oldbourne Press, London (1956). This book contains more than a hundred folds, and is ideal for the beginner. Illustrated by Rolf Harris.

RANDLETT, Samuel. *The Art of Origami*, E. P. Dutton Inc., New York (1961).
A really fine book for both beginner and expert. Traditional and original folds are superbly illustrated by Jean Randlett.

— *The Best of Origami; New Models by Contemporary Folders*, E. P. Dutton, Inc., New York (1963).
This book is an absolute 'must'. The models are quite outstanding, and the material in this book cannot be found elsewhere. Perfect in every way.

LEWIS, Shari, and OPPENHEIMER, Lillian. *Folding Paper Puppets; Folding Paper Toys*, Stein and Day, New York. Puppets (1962), Toys (1963).
Here are two beautifully illustrated books (obtainable almost everywhere) of simple models that work. Splendid for entertaining the young.

YOSHIZAWA, Akira. Books by this author are printed in Japan and can be obtained from The Origami Centre in New York. Printed in Japanese language, but with detailed illustrations easily understood by the initiated.

HONDA, Isao, Editor, Japan Publications Trading Company Ltd., Central P.O., Box 722, Tokyo, Japan.
Mr. Honda has a great number of books to his credit. They are written in English, and are obtainable almost everywhere.

UCHIYAMA, Okimasa, *Origami Zukan* (Picture Book of Origami), Hikari no Kuni, Tokyo, Japan (1958).
A really fine work on cut and uncut Origami, considered the best book of its kind in Japan. It is not necessary to understand Japanese, as the diagrams and symbols are the standard ones and are sufficiently clear.

SOLORZANO SAGREDO, Vicente, *Papiroflexia Zoomorfica* (2 vols.), Apartado de Correos, 319, Valladolid, Spain.
These two volumes contain 1,000 pages, with more than 3,000 illustrations, many by Ligia Montoya. A knowledge of Spanish is helpful in understanding these books, which are obtainable from the author, price 1,200 pesetas the two.

GIL, Elias Gutierrez, *Papiroflexia*, Logrono: Industrias Graficas, UFA, S.L.
This book is obtainable (price one dollar) from the author, at Instituto Ensenaza Media, Burgos, Spain.

MONTERO, N., *El Mundo de Papel*, Valladolid: Editorian Sever-Cuesta (1939).
Available from the author, at Plaza Campillo 3, Valladolid, Spain, price one dollar.

SALVATELLA, Miguel (editor), *Un Hoja de Papel*.
A fine collection of 80 models in illustrations only. Obtainable from the author, at Santo Domingo 5, Barcelona, Spain, price one dollar.

Most booksellers and big stores seem to stock a few Origami books, and it is a good idea to build up a small library by seeing what one can find in the shops.